CLASS

Classic Love

◆

Timeless Wisdom
from Classic Writers

Compiled by Robert Backhouse

Hodder & Stoughton
LONDON SYDNEY AUCKLAND

Copyright © 1995 by Robert Backhouse.

First published in Great Britain 1995.

The right of Robert Backhouse to be identified as the compiler
of the Work has been asserted by him in accordance with the
Copyright, Designs and Patents Act 1988.

10 9 8 7 6 5 4 3 2 1

British Library Cataloguing in Publication Data
A record for this book is available from the British Library

ISBN 0 340 63049 3

Designed and typeset by Watermark, Norfolk

Printed and bound in Great Britain by
Cox & Wyman Ltd, Reading, Berks.

Hodder and Stoughton Ltd
A Division of Hodder Headline PLC
338 Euston Road
London NW1 3BH

Contents

Introduction

What images come to mind when the word love is mentioned?
Romance and sex are top of the list if the tabloids are to be
believed. Emotional love is certainly one of God's great gifts
and included in this collection are two ancient love poems.
They come from the Song of Songs. Some people have inter-
preted this little-read Bible book as an allegory of God's love
for his people, although others have been happy to take the
Song of Songs at face value as a series of love poems.

Some images conjured up by the word 'love' are not so positive. Perhaps one which is often hard to articulate because it is
so personal is lovelessness. It is easy to be critical about other
people's lack of love, but it is much harder to talk about, let
alone take positive action over, our own lovelessness. Where
can encouragement be found? How can we best show love to
others?

I once met a woman who held an unrivalled position of
leadership and responsibility in Christian circles. Yet she was
the first to admit that no matter how much she longed to be
loving, she found herself to be touchy, tactless and often down-
right unloving. At a meeting at which a wise leader had agreed
to answer any questions handed in before he spoke, this
woman's question was: 'I often don't feel at all loving. How
can I be more loving?' The answer given can be summarised,
'You are loved by God. The more you realise that God loves
you the more loving you will be.'

Classic Love includes extracts from many of the great
Christian classic writers who have been revered through the
centuries, and whose timeless wisdom is being sought afresh
today. Some of these men and women, from a wide variety of

countries and Christian traditions, are regarded as saints. None of them is included merely because he or she is a known 'name', but because what was written even hundreds of years ago still speaks to our hearts and minds today. Read Teresa of Avila and C. S. Lewis on loving other people, Bernard of Clairvaux on the assurance of God's constant love, Thomas à Kempis on the qualities of love and fine hymns by Wesley and poetry by George Herbert. These are just a few examples of the rich heritage left by generations of Christian writers, a splendid source of promise and inspiration to draw on today.

Robert Backhouse
Norwich 1995

PART ONE

LOVE FROM GOD

See how much the Father has loved us!
His love is so great that
we are called God's children.
(1 John 3:1, GNB)

Divine love

Expand my heart with Love, that I may feel its transforming power, and may be dissolved in its holy fire.

Let me be possessed by Love, and ravished from myself by fervour and ecstasy!

Let the lover's song be mine, 'I will follow my Beloved on high.'

Let my soul rejoice exceedingly in Love, and lose itself in praise.

Let me love thee more than myself; let me love myself only for thy sake; and in thee love all others; as that perfect law requires, which is a ray of infinite Love that shines in Thee.

I bless thee, O heavenly Father, the Father of my Lord Jesus Christ, that you have remembered such a poor and helpless creature.

The Imitation of Christ, ascribed to Thomas à Kempis

The divine embrace

The end I have in view is the divine Embracing, the union of the soul with the divine Substance. In this loving, obscure knowledge God unites himself with the soul eminently and divinely.

St John of the Cross, *The Dark Night of the Soul*

Love divine

Love Divine, all loves excelling,
Joy of heaven, to earth come down,
Fix in us thy humble dwelling,
All thy faithful mercies crown.
Jesu, thou art all compassion,
Pure unbounded love thou art;
Visit us with thy salvation,
Enter every trembling heart.

Come, almighty to deliver,
Let us all thy life receive;
Suddenly return, and never,
Never more thy temples leave.
Thee we would be always blessing,
Serve thee as thy hosts above,
Pray, and praise thee, without ceasing,
Glory in thy perfect love.

Finish then thy new creation,
Pure and spotless let us be;
Let us see thy great salvation,
Perfectly restored in thee,
Changed from glory into glory,
Till in heaven we take our place,
Till we cast our crowns before thee,
Lost in wonder, love, and praise!
Charles Wesley

Knowing God

Knowledge of God consists in a certain contact of the soul with the Divinity, and it is God himself who is then felt and tasted, though not manifestly and distinctly, as it will be in glory. But this touch of knowledge and of sweetness is so deep and so profound that it penetrates into the inmost substance of the soul. This knowledge savours in some measure of the divine Essence and of everlasting life.

A most sublime and sweet knowledge of God and of his attributes overflows into the understanding from the contact of the attributes of God with the substance of the soul.

St John of the Cross, *The Dark Night of the Soul*

Light and truth

Oh, send thy light and thy truth,
that I may live always near to thee, my God.
Oh, let me feel thy love,
that I may be, as it were, already in heaven,
that I may do all my work as the angels do theirs:
and oh, let me be ready for every work!
Be ready to go out or go in,
to stay or depart just as thou shalt appoint;
Lord, let me have no will of my own,
nor consider my true happiness as depending in the smallest degree on anything that can befall me outwardly,
but as consisting altogether in conformity to thy will.
Amen.

Henry Martyn, *Journal*

The strife of love

In the storm of love two spirits strive together: the Spirit of God and our own spirit. God, through the Holy Spirit, inclines himself towards us, and thereby we are touched in love. And our spirit, by God's working and by the power of love, presses and inclines itself into God; and thereby God is touched. From these two contacts there arises the strife of love, as the very deeps of this meeting; and in that most inward and ardent encounter each spirit is deeply wounded by love. Our own spirit and the Spirit of God sparkle and shine into one another, and each shows to the other its face. This makes each of the spirits yearn for the other in love. Each demands of the other all that it is; and each offers to the other all that it is, and invites it to all that it is. This makes the lovers melt into each other.

God's touch and his gifts, our loving craving and our giving back: these fulfil love. This flux and reflux causes the fountain of love to brim over: and thus the touch of God and our loving craving become one simple love. Thereby the spirit is burned up in the fire of love, and enters so deeply into the touch of God, that it is overcome in all its cravings, and turned to nought in all its works, and empties itself.

John of Ruysbroeck, *The Spiritual Espousals*

Made happy by love

Every lover is assimilated to his beloved. Love makes the loving one become like the thing he loves. God (and his creatures) is not beyond or against being loved. On the contrary, he gladly admits he wants to be loved and be made happy by love.

Richard Rolle, *The Fire of Love*

Transforming love

Love is indeed a transforming force, diffusive and binding: diffusive, because it radiates its beams of goodness not only to friends and neighbours, but also to strangers and enemies; binding, because it makes the lovers one in disposition and will and makes every holy soul one with Christ. For the person who clings to God is one with him in spirit (1 Corinthians 6:17), not by nature, but by grace and identity of will. Love also possesses a transforming force, because it transforms the loving one into the Beloved, lifting him into himself. In fact, the Holy Spirit's fire consumes the heart of the one it enters, and, as it were, turns it into fire, changing it into a form that is like God. Otherwise one could not understand the words 'You are "gods"; you are all sons of the Most High' (Psalm 82:6; cf. John 10:34–5).

Richard Rolle, *The Fire of Love*

Like him

Dear friends, now we are children of God, and what we will be has not yet been made known. But we know that when he appears, we shall be like him, for we shall see him as he is.

1 John 3:2, NIV

The bridle of love

Penitential practices, among other things, were instituted for a special object. Fasting, watching, praying, kneeling, scourging, wearing hair shirts, sleeping on a hard surface, or whatever it may be, were all invented because body and flesh are always in opposition to spirit. Since the body is always far too strong for the spirit, battle is always joined between them, it is a never-ending conflict. Here the body is bold and strong, for here it is at home; the world helps it, the earth is its fatherland. It is aided by all its family: food, drink, ease – all are opposed to spirit. The spirit is an alien here. Its family, its whole race, are in heaven; there its loved ones dwell. To aid the spirit in its distress, and to impede the flesh slightly in this battle, and prevent it conquering the spirit, we put the bridle of penitential practices to it. These help to curb the flesh, so that the spirit may control it. This is done to bring it into subjection. But it is a thousand times more effective to put the bridle of love on it. With love you overcome it most surely, with love you load it most heavily.

God lies in wait for us, therefore, with nothing so much as with love.

Meister Eckhart, *Sermons*

Love descendeth from God

Love is a great thing and a good, and alone maketh heavy burdens light, and beareth in like balance things pleasant and unpleasant; it beareth a heavy burden and feeleth it not, and maketh bitter things to be savoury and sweet. Love will always have his mind upward to God and will not be occupied with love of the world. Nothing, therefore, is more sweet than love, nothing higher, nothing stronger, nothing larger, nothing more joyful, nothing fuller, nor anything better in heaven or earth; for love descendeth from God, and may not rest finally in anything lower than God.

St Francis of Assisi, *Admonitions*

Enfolded in his love

In his love he clothes us, enfolds us and embraces us; that tender love completely surrounds us, never to leave us.

Lady Julian of Norwich, *Revelations of Divine Love*

Assurance of God's love

The Lord says, 'I love those who love me, and those who seek me find me' (Proverbs 8:17).

God assures you of his love if you love him. God also promises to care for you if you keep your relationship strong with him. Are you keeping vigil? Then God will keep vigil, too.

Even if you get up in the middle of the night you will discover that God is already awake, looking out for your arrival. You will be wrong ever to think that you can be one step ahead of God. Souls which are deeply assured of these wonderful truths wonder at the thought that this majestic God can give them so much attention as if God had nobody else to look after.

I want to add just one thing, which although it appears to be incredible is, in fact, true. I direct this especially to those who are spiritually minded among you. A soul which looks at God does so in the same way that God looks at him, as if it was the only soul that God looked at. So the soul gives its full attention to God because God has given his full attention to it. How good you are, O Lord, to the soul which seeks you! You come to it, you embrace it, you reveal yourself as its Bridegroom and its husband. You are its Lord, are above everything and blessed by God for ever. Amen.

St Bernard of Clairvaux, *On Loving God*

The fire of love

This fire of love is not usually experienced straightaway. It does not set fire to the soul because of the impurity of human nature, or because the soul does not know what is happening, and therefore has given itself no opportunity to be peaceful and quiet. Sometimes, however, the soul has a strong longing for God. The more this increases, the more the soul is affected, and set on fire with love towards God. It does not know what is happening or where this love is coming from, it simply sees these flames of love burning higher and higher as it lovingly yearns for God. When David was in this dark night, he described it like this, 'When my heart was grieved and my spirit embittered, I was senseless and ignorant; I was a brute beast before you' (Psalm 73:21–2).

Because my heart was on fire – in contemplative love – my desires and tastes were also transformed. I changed from being sensual to being spiritual. This is the dryness and the cutting off from unspiritual things that we are talking about, and I, David says, was senseless and ignorant. For the soul without being aware of what it is doing, finds that it is totally cut off from all spiritual and unspiritual things from which it derives pleasure. It now finds itself absorbed, without knowing how.

Sometimes, the fires of love in the spirit burn with tremendous intensity but the soul's longing for God becomes so great that the person's bones seem to be dried up. The human powers of strength and warmth seem to fade away because of the intensity of this loving seeking after God. The soul believes this thirst of love to be a real thirst. This is the thirst that David had when he said, 'My soul thirsts for God, for the living God' (Psalm 42:2).

St John of the Cross, *The Dark Night of the Soul*

'God so loved the world . . .'

O sacred head, sore wounded,
  Defiled and put to scorn;
O kingly head, surrounded
  With mocking crown of thorn:
What sorrow mars thy grandeur?
  Can death thy bloom deflower?
O countenance whose splendour
  The hosts of heaven adore.

I pray thee, Jesus, own me,
  Me, Shepherd good, for thine;
Who to thy fold hast won me,
  And fed with truth divine.
Me guilty, me refuse not,
  Incline thy face to me,
This comfort that I lose not,
  On earth to comfort thee.

In thy most bitter passion
  My heart to share doth cry,
With thee for my salvation
  Upon the Cross to die.
Ah, keep my heart thus movèd
  To stand thy Cross beneath,
To mourn thee, well-belovèd,
  Yet thank thee for thy death.

Paul Gerhardt

Contemplatives

Contemplatives are highly charged with the love of eternity. They are, in fact, so far above others in their sweet state of loving and being loved of God that they rarely, if ever, engage in worldly affairs, or become involved with ecclesiastical rank or honour. They keep themselves to themselves. Alone, they ascend. Their minds constant in Christ, they joyfully sing songs of praise.

This is the order the church follows, where the highest angels are not sent out, but always remain near God. Similarly, those highest in love and contemplation of Christ attend directly to divine things. They do not become involved with rank among people; such activity being reserved for those who are preoccupied with outward human affairs, and are less concerned with the joys of inward things.

So, each man's state is preordained by God. While some may be elected to church orders, others are free to remain alone with God. And in this calling, God raises those chosen to abandon all external occupation. These people are the holiest, yet the lowest of men. They dwell within themselves, rarely moving out to work miracles.

Richard Rolle, *The Fire of Love*

Contemplation

Contemplation is nothing else but a secret, peaceful, and loving infusion of God, which if admitted, will set the soul on fire with the spirit of love.

St John of the Cross, *The Dark Night of the Soul*

God's all-knowing love

Lord, I know not what I ought to ask of you; only you know what we need; you love me better than I know how to love myself. O Father, give to your child that which he himself knows not how to ask. I dare not ask either for crosses or consolations; I simply present myself before you; I open my heart to you. Behold my needs which I know not myself; see, and do according to your tender mercy. Smite, or heal; depress me, or raise me up; I adore all your purposes without knowing them; I am silent; I offer myself in sacrifice; I yield myself to you; I would have no other desire than to accomplish your will. Teach me to pray; pray yourself in me.

François Fénelon, *Christian Perfection*

Three stages of growth

There are three stages of growth in maturity.
Love of self for self's sake;
Love of God for self's sake;
Love of God for God.

St Bernard of Clairvaux, *On Loving God*

Love and creation

To know that Love alone was the beginning of nature and creation, that nothing but Love encompasses the whole universe of things, that the governing hand that overrules all, the watchful Eye that sees through all, is nothing but omnipotent and omniscient Love, using an infinity of wisdom, to save every misguided creature from the miserable works of his own hands, and make happiness and glory the perpetual inheritance of all the creation, is a reflection that must be quite ravishing to every intelligent creature that is sensible of it.

William Law, *A Serious Call to a Devout and Holy Life*

Look out on the world around you. What witness does it bear concerning the God who made it? Who made the sunshine, and the flowers, and singing birds, the little children, and all that causes the joy of this life? God is love, and he that dwelleth in love dwelleth in God, and God in him. But if, in spite of many bad habits, we desire to get rid of our bad habits; if, in spite of many faults, we still desire to be faultless and perfect; if, in spite of many weaknesses, we still desire to be strong; if, in one word, we still hunger and thirst after righteousness, and long to be good men; then, in due time, the love of God will be shed abroad in our hearts by the Holy Spirit.

Charles Kingsley, *Apologia pro Vita Sua*

The third grade of love

The third grade of love is when the mind of man is rapt into the abyss of divine light, so that, utterly oblivious of all exterior things, it knows not itself and passes wholly into its God. And so in this state is held in check and lulled to deep sleep the crowd of carnal desires.

In this state, while the mind is alienated from itself, while it is rapt in the secret closet of the divine privacy, while it is on all sides encircled by the conflagration of divine love, and is intimately penetrated and set on fire through and through, it strips off self and puts on a certain divine condition, and being configured to the beauty gazed upon, it passes into a new kind of glory.

Richard of St-Victor, *Benjamin Major*

God's love

God's love is like the River Amazon flowing down to water one daisy.

Anonymous

God is love

'God is love.' Yes – in that by his love he compels all who can love and all who do love to love him.

Secondly, God is love in that every God-created and loving thing compels him by its love to love it, willy-nilly.

Thirdly, God is love in that his love drives all his lovers out of multiplicity. The love of God in multiplicity pursues the love which is himself right out of multiplicity into his very unity.

Fourthly, God is love who, by his love, provides all creatures with their life and being, preserving them in his love. Just as the colour of cloth is preserved in the cloth, so creatures are preserved in existence by love, that is, God. Take the colour from cloth, and its being is gone; so creatures all lose their being if taken from love, that is, from God. God is love, and so lovely is he that lovers all love him, willy-nilly. No creature is so vile that it loves what is bad. What we love must be good or must seem to be good. But creaturely good, all told, is rank evil compared with God.

St Augustine says, 'Love, that in meditating love you may provide the means to satisfy your soul.' God is love.

My children, pay attention to me, I beg. Know this. God loves my soul so much that whether he wishes it or not, his very life and being depend upon his loving me. To stop God loving me would be to rob him of his Godhead, for God is love no less than he is truth. As he is good, so he is love as well. This is the absolute truth, as God lives.

Meister Eckhart, *Sermons*

New every morning is God's love

New every morning is God's love
Our wakening and uprising prove;
Through sleep and darkness safely brought,
Restored to life, and power, and thought.

New mercies, each returning day,
Hover around us while we pray;
New perils past, new sins forgiven,
New thoughts of God, new hopes of heaven.

If on our daily course our mind
Be set to hallow all we find,
New treasures still, of countless price,
God will provide for sacrifice.

The trivial round, the common task,
Would furnish all we ought to ask,
Room to deny ourselves, a road
To bring us daily nearer God.

Only, O Lord, in thy dear love
Fit us for perfect rest above;
And help us this and every day
To live more nearly as we pray.

John Keble

Mercy, Pity, Peace and Love

To Mercy, Pity, Peace, and Love,
All pray in their distress,
And to these virtues of delight
Return their thankfulness.

For Mercy, Pity, Peace, and Love,
Is God our Father dear;
And Mercy, Pity, Peace, and Love,
Is Man, his child and care.

For Mercy has a human heart,
Pity, a human face;
And Love, the human form divine,
And Peace, the human dress.

Then every man, of every clime,
That prays in his distress,
Prays to the human form divine:
Love, Mercy, Pity, Peace.

William Blake

Light is love

The light is love, which God in his wisdom measures out to us in the best way for us.

The light is not bright enough to enable us to see our most happy day, but neither is that day totally obscured. We have enough light to live a rewarding life of hard work that earns the endless praise of God. I saw this in the sixth Revelation, where the Lord said, 'I thank you for all your service and hard work.' So love keeps us in faith and hope, and hope leads us in love. And in the end all will be love.

I understood this light of love in three ways. First, uncreated love; second, created love; third, given love. Uncreated love is God; created love is our soul in God; given love is virtue. Given love is a precious gift which God works in us. Through it we love God for himself, we love ourselves in God; and we love everything which God loves, for his sake.

Lady Julian of Norwich, *Revelations of Divine Love*

The Divine Lover

Me, Lord? Canst thou misspend
One word, misplace one look on me?
Call'st me thy Love, thy Friend?
Can this poor soul the object be
Of these love-glances, those life-kindling eyes?
What? I the centre of thy arms' embraces?
Of all thy labour I the prize?
Love never mocks, Truth never lies.
Oh how I quake: Hope fear, fear hope displaces:
I would, but cannot hope: such wondrous love amazes.

Phineas Fletcher, *Poems*

Myrrh

God takes a thousand times more pains with us than the artist with his picture, by many touches of sorrow, and by many colours of circumstance, to bring man into the form which is the highest and noblest in his sight, if only we received his gifts and myrrh in the right spirit.

But when the cup is put away, and these feelings are stifled or unheeded, a greater injury is done to the soul than can ever be amended. For no heart can conceive in what surpassing love God gives us this myrrh; yet this which we ought to receive to our soul's good, we allow to pass by us in our sleepy indifference, and nothing comes of it. Then we come and complain: 'Alas, Lord! I am so dry, and it is so dark within me!' I tell you, dear child, open your heart to the pain, and it will do you more good than if you were full of feeling and devoutness.

Johann Tauler, *Sermons*

Sow in tears, reap in joy

Those who sow in tears will reap with songs of joy. He who goes out weeping, carrying seed to sow, will return with songs of joy, carrying sheaves with him.

Psalm 126:5–6, NIV

God's love and grace

If you knew the whole Bible by heart and all the teachings of
the philosophers, how would this help you without the grace
and love of God?

The Imitation of Christ, ascribed to Thomas à Kempis

PART TWO

LOVE FROM JESUS CHRIST

This is love:
not that we loved God, but that he loved us
and sent his Son as an atoning sacrifice for our sins.
(1 John 4:10, NIV)

Spiritual understanding

It was at that time that the Lord gave me a spiritual understanding of the warm friendliness of his love. I saw that he is everything which is good and comfortable. He is our clothing: out of love for us he wraps us around, fastens the clasp, and enfolds us in his love, so that he will never leave us. I saw that he is everything that is good for us.

Lady Julian of Norwich, *Revelations of Divine Love*

The name of Jesus

How sweet the name of Jesus sounds
In a believer's ear!
It soothes his sorrows, heals his wounds,
And drives away his fear.

It makes the wounded spirit whole,
And calms the troubled breast;
'Tis manna to the hungry soul,
And to the weary rest.

John Newton

Love lives

Love lives beyond
The tomb, the earth, which fades like dew!
I love the fond,
The faithful and the true.

Love lives in sleep,
The happiness of healthy dreams:
Eve's dews may weep
But love delightful seems.

'Tis seen in flowers
And in the morning's pearly dew;
In earth's green hours
And in the heaven's eternal blue.

John Clare

Love bade me welcome

Love bade me welcome; yet my soul drew back,
    Guiltie of dust and sinne.
But quick-ey'd Love, observing me grow slack
    From my first entrance in,
Drew nearer to me, sweetly questioning,
    If I lack'd any thing.

A guest, I answer'd, worthy to be here:
    Love said, You shall be he.
I the unkinde, ungrateful? Ah my deare,
    I cannot look on thee.
Love took my hand, and smiling did reply,
    Who make the eyes but I?

Truth Lord, but I have marr'd them: let my shame
    Go where it doth deserve.
And know you not, sayes Love, who bore the blame?
    My desire, then I will serve.
You must sit down, sayes Love, and taste my meat:
    So I did sit and eat.

George Herbert

Love's desire

I am nothing, I have nothing. I desire nothing but the love of
Jesus in Jerusalem.

Walter Hilton, *The Scale of Perfection*

My song is love unknown

My song is love unknown,
My Saviour's love to me,
Love to the loveless shown,
That they might lovely be.
O, who am I,
That for my sake
My Lord should take
Frail flesh, and die?

He came from his blest throne,
Salvation to bestow:
But men made strange, and none
The longed-for Christ would know.
But O, my Friend,
My Friend indeed,
Who at my need
His life did spend!

Here might I stay and sing,
No story so divine;
Never was love, dear King,
Never was grief like thine!
This is my Friend,
In whose sweet praise
I all my days
Could gladly spend.

Samuel Crossman

It is a thing most wonderful

It is a thing most wonderful,
Almost too wonderful to be,
That God's own Son should come from heaven,
And die to save a child like me.

And yet I know that it is true:
He chose a poor and humble lot,
And wept, and toiled, and mourned, and died
For love of those who loved him not.

But even could I see him die,
I could but see a little part
Of that great love, which, like a fire,
Is always burning in his heart.

It is most wonderful to know
His love for me so free and sure;
But 'tis more wonderful to see
My love for him so faint and poor.

And yet I want to love thee, Lord;
O light the flame within my heart,
And I will love thee more and more,
Until I see thee as thou art.

W. Walsham How

God's demonstration

God demonstrates his own love for us in this: While we were
still sinners, Christ died for us.

Romans 5:8, NIV

The love of Jesus

The love of Jesus is a noble love. It continually looks up to heaven and abhors the restraints of its earthly prison. This love surpasses all sweetness, strength, height, depth, and breadth: nothing is more pleasing, nothing more full, nothing more excellent in heaven, or on earth. For 'love is born of God'. It cannot find rest in created things, but rests only in God from whom it is derived.

The Imitation of Christ, ascribed to Thomas à Kempis

Jesu, Lover of my soul

Jesu, Lover of my soul,
    Let me to thy bosom fly,
While the nearer waters roll,
    While the tempest still is high:
Hide me, O my Saviour, hide,
    Till the storm of life be past!
Safe into the haven guide,
    Oh, receive my soul at last!

Other refuge have I none,
    Hangs my helpless soul on thee;
Leave, ah! leave me not alone,
    Still support and comfort me:
All my trust on thee is stayed,
    All my help from thee I bring;
Cover my defenceless head
    With the shadow of thy wing.

Charles Wesley

O quench my soul in Love!

Love, Love, O Love, I am no longer I:
Love, Love, O Love, thyself so utterly
   Thou giv'st me, Jesu, that I can but die.
Love, O Love, I am possessed of thee,
   Love, Love, my Love, O take me in a sigh!
   Love, glad and spent I lie.
     O Love, my Bliss,
     O Lover's Kiss!
   O quench my soul in Love!

Jacopone da Todi, *Poems*

Love was my meaning

From the time of my first showings (visions) I had often wanted to know what was our Lord's meaning. It was more than fifteen years after that I was answered in my spirit's understanding. 'You would know our Lord's meaning in this thing? Know it well. Love was his meaning. Who showed it you? Love. What did he show you? Love. Why did he show it? For love. Hold on to this and you will know and understand love more and more. But you will not know or learn anything else – ever!'

So it was that I learned that love was our Lord's meaning. And I saw for certain, both here and elsewhere, that before ever he made us, God loved us; and that his love has never slackened, nor ever shall. In this love all his works have been done, and in this love he has made everything serve us; and in this love life is everlasting. Our being was when we were made, but the love in which he made us never had beginning. In it we have our beginning.

All this we shall see in God for ever.

May Jesus grant this. Amen.

Lady Julian of Norwich, *Revelations of Divine Love*

The burning love of Christ

So let us seek that burning love of Christ within us, instead of concerning ourselves with worthless argument. Because while we are preoccupied with our silly questioning minds, we fail to experience the sweetness of eternity. So many people today burn up in the fires of learning and not of love, that love remains unknown. Though all their study is directed to this end – the burning love of God – yet what love is, and how it feels, escapes them! What a pity! An old wife may know more of God's love and the rejection of worldly pleasure than a theologian whose learning is empty because he studies out of pride to appear a fine scholar and be well known, and to gain greater distinctions and hold higher office. Such folk really deserve to be considered not wise men, but fools.

Richard Rolle, *The Fire of Love*

When I survey the wondrous cross

When I survey the wondrous Cross
On which the Prince of Glory died,
My richest gain I count but loss,
And pour contempt on all my pride.

Forbid it, Lord, that I should boast
Save in the death of Christ, my God;
All the vain things that charm me most,
I sacrifice them to his blood.

See from his head, his hands, his feet,
Sorrow and love flow mingled down;
Did e'er such love and sorrow meet?
Or thorns compose so rich a crown?

His dying crimson like a robe
Spreads o'er his body on the Tree,
Then am I dead to all the globe,
And all the globe is dead to me.

Were the whole realm of nature mine,
That were a present far too small;
Love so amazing, so divine,
Demands my soul, my life, my all.

Isaac Watts

Carrying the cross

Carrying his own cross, he went out to the place of the Skull
(which in Aramaic is called Golgotha).

John 19:17, NIV

PART THREE

LOVE FOR GOD

[Jesus said,] 'She has poured perfume on my feet.
Therefore, I tell you, her many sins
have been forgiven – for
she loved much.
But he who has been forgiven little
loves little.'
(Luke 7:46–7, NIV)

Three ways to love God

It has been said that Christ's love is tender, wise and strong. I say that it is tender, since he has taken on himself our human nature; wise because he has kept himself free from all sin; and strong because he came to the point of enduring death.

From the way in which Christ lived you can learn, Christian friend, how you should love Christ. Learn to love him tenderly, to love him wisely and to love him with strong powerful love.

If you love Christ tenderly you will not be enticed away from him; if you love Christ wisely you will not be deceived and so drawn away from him; if you love Christ powerfully nothing will be able to separate you from him. Take delight in Christ for he is wisdom above everything else. Then human glory and sinful human passions will not take you away from him. Let Christ, who is the truth, so enlighten you that you are not drawn away from him by any false spirit.

St Bernard of Clairvaux, *On Loving God*

Let us make God the beginning and end of our love, for he is the fountain from which all good things flow and into him alone they flow back. Let him therefore be the beginning of our love.

Richard Rolle, *The Fire of Love*

My God, I love thee

✷

My God, I love thee, not because
  I hope for heaven thereby,
Nor yet because who love thee not
  Are lost eternally.

Thou, O my Jesus, thou didst me
  Upon the Cross embrace;
For me didst bear the nails and spear,
  And manifold disgrace,

And griefs and torments numberless
  And sweat of agony;
E'en death itself; and all for one
  Who was thine enemy.

Then why, O blessed Jesus Christ,
  Should I not love thee well,
Not for the sake of winning heaven,
  Or of escaping hell;

Not with the hope of gaining aught
  Not seeking a reward;
But as thyself hast loved me,
  O ever-loving Lord!

E'en so I love thee, and will love,
  And in thy praise will sing,
Solely because thou art my God,
  And my eternal King.

17th-century Latin, translated by Edward Caswall

Love of Jesus above all

Blessed is the man who knows what it is to love Jesus, and for his sake to despise himself. To preserve this love, he must relinquish the love of himself and of all creatures; for Jesus will be loved alone. To love the creatures is deceitful and unstable: to love Jesus is being faithful and lasts for ever. The person who follows the creature must fail when the creature fails; but he who follows Jesus, will live for ever.

Love Jesus and retain him as your friend; for, though the heavens and the earth should be destroyed, he will not forsake you, or allow you to perish. One day you must be separated from all created things, whether you desire this or not. Whether you live or die, follow Jesus. Firmly commit yourself to his faithful protection, who, when all earthly sources fail, is alone able to sustain you.

The Imitation of Christ, ascribed to Thomas à Kempis

Take my love

Take my love; my Lord, I pour
At Thy feet its treasure-store,
Take myself, and I will be
Ever, only, all for Thee!

Frances R. Havergal

Love for God

Love the Lord your God with all your heart, with all your soul, and with all your mind.

Matthew 22:37, GNB

The person who loves God is known by him.

1 Corinthians 8:3, GNB

We know that in all things God works for good with those who love him, those whom he has called according to his purpose.

Romans 8:28, GNB

Man is the perfection of the universe; the spirit is the perfection of man; love is the perfection of the spirit; and charity the perfection of love. Hence, the love of God is the goal, the perfection and the crown of the whole universe.

St François de Sales, *Introduction to a Devout Life*

God does not need us to say many words to him, nor to think many thoughts. He sees our hearts, and that is enough for him. He sees very well our suffering and our submission. We have only to repeat continuously to a person we love, 'I love you with all my heart.' It even happens, often, that we go a long time without thinking that we love him, and we love him no less during this period than in those in which we make him the most tender protestations. True love rests in the depths of the heart.

François Fénelon, *Christian Perfection*

Wholehearted love for God

Give me a person who wholeheartedly loves God above everything else, a person who loves both himself and his neighbour
to the same extent that God loves each of them. Give me a person who loves his enemy like a person who may at some time
in the future turn to the love of God, a person who naturally
loves his human relations very tenderly, but who loves his
spiritual parents, that is those who have taught him the Christian faith, even more abundantly because of God's grace. This
person's love for everything else is governed by his love for
God. He despises the earth and looks up to heaven. He uses
this world, but does not abuse it. On account of an inner
faculty of his soul he knows how to distinguish between the
things which should be chosen and loved and the things that
should be just used. He makes use of transitory things for his
journey through this life while he embraces with everlasting
joy the things of eternity. Show me, I ask, a person who does
this and I will be bold enough to declare that he is wise. He sees
things as they really are and is able with truth and confidence
to boast, 'his banner over me is love' (Song of Songs 2:4).
St Bernard of Clairvaux, *The Song of Songs*

Daughter, if you knew how sweet your love is to me, you
would never do anything else but love me with all your heart.
St Catherine of Siena, *Dialogo*

St Francis' passionate love

○

No human tongue could describe the passionate love with which Francis turned to Christ, his Spouse. He seemed to be completely absorbed by the fire of divine love like a glowing coal.

The memory of Christ Jesus crucified was ever present in the depths of his heart like a bundle of myrrh, and he longed to be wholly transformed into him by the fire of his love.

He loved Christ so fervently, and Christ returned his love so intimately, that he seemed to have his Saviour before his eyes continually, as he once privately admitted to his companions.

St Bonaventura, *The Life of St Francis*

Humility, patience and love of God

There is no love of God without patience, and no patience without lowliness and sweetness of spirit.

Humility and patience are the surest proofs of the increase of love.

Humility alone unites patience with love, without which it is impossible to draw profit from suffering, or, indeed, to avoid complaint, especially when we think we have given no occasion for what men make us suffer.

True humility is a kind of self-annihilation, and this is the centre of all virtues.

A soul returned to God ought to be attentive to everything which is said to him on the subject of salvation with a desire to profit thereby.

Of the sins which God has pardoned, let nothing remain but a deeper humility in the heart, and a stricter regulation in our words, in our actions, and in our sufferings.

John Wesley, *A Plain Man's Guide to Holiness*

Christian morality

✺

The God of the Christians is a God who makes the soul aware that he is its only good. In him alone it can find peace. Only in loving him can it find joy. He is a God who at the same time fills the soul with loathing for those things that hold it back and thus prevent it from loving God with all its might. Self-love and lust, which keep it back, are intolerable. So God makes the soul aware of this underlying self-love which destroys it. He alone can cure it.

Blaise Pascal, *Pensées*

✺

Doing God's will with love

That piety which sanctifies us, and which is a true devotion to God, consists in doing all his will precisely at the time, in the situation, and under the circumstances, in which he has placed us. Perfect devotedness requires, not only that we do the will of God, but that we do it with love. God would have us serve him with delight; it is our hearts that he asks of us.

François Fénelon, *Christian Perfection*

Bathed in the essence of God

When through love the soul goes beyond all working of the intellect and all images in the mind, and is rapt above itself, utterly leaving itself, it flows into God: then is God its peace and fullness.

It loses itself in the infinite solitude and darkness of the Godhead; but so to lose itself is rather to find itself. This soul is, as it were, all God-coloured, because its essence is bathed in the Essence of God.

Abbot Louis of Blois, *Meditations*

The soul is a tree existing by love

The soul is a tree existing by love, and can live by nothing else but love. If this soul have not in truth the divine love of perfect charity she cannot produce the fruit of life, but only of death. So this tree's roots, that is the affection of the soul, should grow in and issue from the circle of true self-knowledge which is contained in Me, who have neither beginning nor end, like the circumference of a circle. No matter how you turn in a circle, because a circumference has no beginning and no end, you will always remain in the circle. And this knowledge of yourself and of Me is found in the earth of true humility, which is as wide as the diameter of the circle, that is, the knowledge of self and of Me.

St Catherine of Siena, *Dialogo*

God, the love of your heart

For silence is not God, nor speaking; fasting is not God, nor eating; solitude is not God, nor company; nor any other pair of opposites. He is hidden between them, and cannot be found by anything your soul does, but only by the love of your heart. He cannot be known by reason, he cannot be thought, caught, or sought by understanding. But he can be loved and chosen by the true, loving will of your heart.

If God is your love and your purpose, the chief aim of your heart, it is all you need in this life, although you never see more of him with the eye of reason your whole life long. Such a blind shot with the sharp dart of longing love will never miss its mark, which is God.

Anonymous, *The Cloud of Unknowing*

Loving creation

✺

Beauty is God's handwriting. Welcome it in every fair face, every fair day, every fair flower.

Charles Kingsley, *Apologia pro Vita Sua*

✺

But what do I love when I love thee? Not grace of bodies, nor the beauty of the seasons, nor the brightness of the light . . . nor inexhaustible melodies of sweet song, nor the fragrant smell of flowers, of ointments and spices. . . . None of these love I when I love my God: and yet I love a kind of light, and of melody and of fragrance . . . when I love my God. . . .

And what is this? I asked the earth and it said, 'I am not He:' and whatsoever is in it confessed the same.

I asked the sea and the deeps, and all that swimming or creeping life therein, and they answered, 'We are not thy God, seek above us.'

I asked the wandering winds; and the whole air with his inhabitants spoke 'I am not God.'

I asked the heavens, sun, moon and stars, 'Nor (say they) are we the God whom thou seekest.'

And I replied unto all those things which encompass the door of my flesh, 'Ye have told me of my God, that ye are not He: tell me something of Him.'

And they cried all with a great voice, 'He made us.' My questioning them was my mind's desire, and their Beauty was their answer.

St Augustine, *Confessions*

Late have I loved Thee

Late have I loved Thee, O Beauty so ancient and so new; late have I loved Thee! For behold Thou wert within me, and I outside; and I sought Thee outside and in my unloveliness fell upon those lovely things that Thou hast made. Thou wert with me and I was not with Thee. I was kept from Thee by those things, yet had they not been in Thee, they would not have been at all. Thou didst call and cry to me and break upon my deafness: and Thou didst send forth Thy beams and shine upon me and chase away my blindness: Thou didst breathe fragrance upon me, and I drew in my breath and do now pant for Thee: I tasted Thee, and now hunger and thirst for Thee: Thou didst touch me, and I have burned for Thy peace.

St Augustine, *Confessions*

Loving God for himself

What a wonderful and noble thing it is to speak about the love of God. Nobody is able to speak perfectly about the smallest facet of his love. You can only give superficial illustrations as God's love is beyond man's understanding. This is what I mean when I say that we are to love God with a chaste love, to love God for himself, and not for anything we may receive. When a soul is in the presence of God, the clear beam of everlasting light illumines his understanding. The soul sees and feels the blessedness of God himself. He is unaware of any of God's kindnesses. All he sees and feels is God himself. So, while we speak about the great goodness and the great kindness that God has shown us in this life, a perfect lover of God will have no other reason to love God, than God himself.

The Epistle of Prayer (14th century)

Pure love comes to God himself, to abide in him, but not to seek anything from him.

St Thomas Aquinas, *Summa Theologiae*

Wholly obtain the love of Jesus

❉

A real pilgrim going to Jerusalem leaves his house and land, wife and children; he divests himself of all that he possesses in order to travel light and without encumbrance. Similarly, if you wish to be a spiritual pilgrim, you must divest yourself of all that you possess; that is, both of good deeds and bad, and leave them all behind you.

Recognize your own poverty, so that you will not place any confidence in your own work; instead, always be desiring the grace of deeper love, and seeking the spiritual presence of Jesus. If you do this, you will be setting your heart wholly on obtaining the love of Jesus and whatever spiritual vision of himself that he is willing to grant, for it is to this end alone that you have been created and redeemed; this is your beginning and your end, your joy and your bliss. Therefore, whatever you may possess, and however fruitful your activities, regard them all as worthless without the inward certainty and experience of this love. Keep this intention constantly in mind and hold to it firmly; it will sustain you among all the perils of your pilgrimage.

Walter Hilton, *The Scale of Perfection*

Pure love

You may keep on being drawn into loving God for the sake of sweet feelings. You will know that this has happened if you start complaining when these feelings are absent. If you do, your love is not yet pure and perfect. For pure perfect love, though it agrees that the body is sustained and comforted when such feelings or fears are present, never grumbles when without them; it is just as pleased not to have those consolations, if it is God's will.

While in some people comfort and consolation is the norm, in others it is rare. It is entirely a matter of God's purpose and plan, according to the needs of each individual. Some people are so spiritually weak and sensitive that, if they did not receive God's comfort, they would find it impossible to bear the various temptations and tribulations which they have to suffer and endure in this life, and which come from their physical and spiritual foes. There are those who are so frail physically that they are unable to perform the penance needed for forgiveness. These people will be cleansed by our Lord, in his grace, with sweet emotions and tears. Then there are those, on the other hand, who are so strong in spirit that they glean all the comfort they require from within their own souls and have little need to be sustained with sweet emotions. They remain strong by offering up their reverent, humble outreach of love and obedient will. Which of the two is holier or dearer to God is not for me to say. God alone knows.

The Cloud of Unknowing

O for a heart to praise my God

O for a heart to praise my God,
A heart from sin set free;
A heart that always feels thy blood
So freely spilt for me:

A heart resigned, submissive, meek,
My dear Redeemer's throne;
Where only Christ is heard to speak,
Where Jesus reigns alone:

A humble, lowly, contrite heart,
Believing, true, and clean,
Which neither life nor death can part
From him that dwells within:

A heart in every thought renewed,
And full of love divine;
Perfect and right and pure and good,
A copy, Lord, of thine.

My heart, thou know'st, can never rest
Till thou create my peace;
Till of mine Eden repossest,
From self, and sin, I cease.

Thy nature, gracious Lord, impart,
Come quickly from above;
Write thy new name upon my heart,
Thy new best name of love.

Charles Wesley

Loving God

This is love: not that we loved God, but that he loved us and sent his Son as an atoning sacrifice for our sins. Dear friends, since God so loved us, we also ought to love one another. No-one has ever seen God; but if we love one another, God lives in us and his love is made complete in us.

1 John 4:10–12, NIV

He has loved us without being loved. We are bound to him, and not he to us, because before he was loved, he loved us and created us. There it is, then: we cannot love him with this first love. Yet I say that God demands of us, that as he has loved us without any second thoughts, so he should be loved by us.

In what way can we do this? I tell you, through a means which he established, by which we can love him freely. That is, we can be useful, not to him, which is impossible, but to our neighbour. To show the love that we have for him, we ought to serve and love every rational creature and extend our charity to good and bad, as much as to one who does us ill service and criticises us as to one who serves us. For God's charity extends over just men and sinners.

St Catherine of Siena, *Dialogo*

God's will as love

❋

Our love of God must not be gauged by the passing feelings we experience that are not controlled by the will, but rather we must judge them by the enduring quality of the will itself. For loving God means that we join our will to God's will. It means that our will consents to whatever the will of God commands. It means that we have only one reason for wishing anything, and the reason is that we know that God wills it.

The visitations of God's grace that come to us in the form of feelings and emotions, are for God to bestow when and where and to whom he wills. It is not for us to seek them, or even to ask for them, and if God should suddenly remove them from us, our wills must be in agreement with his. For the man who loves God is the man who bears patiently with all that God does to him, and who is zealous in carrying out God's purposes.

Aelred of Rievaulx, *Sermons*

❋

Fire is the symbol of love; and the love of God is the principle and the end of all our good works.

John Wesley, *The Plain Man's Guide to Holiness*

Loving God, loving the world

While the love of this world's things dominates a person's heart, it makes him lack inner devotion. It is so true that the love of God and the love of this world are mutually exclusive. It is impossible for them both to reside in the same soul. Whichever love is stronger drives out the other. It is therefore clear who is the lover of this world and who is the follower of Christ. Ardent love of Christ will act against the world and the flesh, so the lovers of the world will act against God and their own souls.

Richard Rolle, *The Fire of Love*

He who is filled with love is filled with God himself.

St Augustine, *Confessions*

Come down, O love divine

Come down, O love divine,
Seek thou this soul of mine,
And visit it with thine own ardour glowing;
O Comforter, draw near,
Within my heart appear,
And kindle it, thy holy flame bestowing.

O let it freely burn,
Till earthly passions turn
To dust and ashes in its heat consuming;
And let thy glorious light
Shine ever on my sight,
And clothe me round, the while my path illuming.

Let holy charity
Mine outward vesture be,
And lowliness become mine inner clothing;
True lowliness of heart,
Which takes the humbler part,
And o'er its own shortcomings weeps with loathing.

And so the yearning strong,
With which the soul will long,
Shall far outpass the power of human telling;
For none can guess its grace,
Till he become the place
Wherein the Holy Spirit makes his dwelling.

Bianco da Siena, translated by R. F. Littledale

To love God entirely

To love God entirely, the soul must be pure and strong, staying faithful to God in times of trouble, alert against dishonesty and fraud. In this way man will not just find the supreme good, he will himself become like the supreme good – because he will be transformed into the image of God.

St Augustine, *The Catholic Church*

Loving Christ

Loving Christ involves three things as far as my studies of Scripture show: warmth, song, sweetness. In my personal experience, these cannot last long without solitude.

These three things – warmth, song and sweetness – are the sign of love's most perfect form. In them total perfection of Christianity is to be found. I, by the grace of Jesus, in my limited, meagre ability, have accepted them. Even so, I would not dare to equate myself with the saints who displayed these gifts, because they were way beyond me in their understanding of such things.

I call heat that point when the mind is fired with eternal love. The heart simply feels itself burning with a real love, not an imaginary one. For the heart, full of fervour and set ablaze, produces a feeling of fiery love.

I call song that point when the soul has an overflowing ardent and sweet feeling of heavenly praise, when thought turns to song, when it is wrapped up in sweet harmony.

Both these things are only perceived in the deepest devotion, not in laziness. From them a third, unutterable sweetness, proceeds. Heat and song cause a marvellous sweetness in the soul, just as they, too, can be produced by sweetness.

Richard Rolle, *The Fire of Love*

PART FOUR

LOVE FOR YOUR NEIGHBOUR

Love your neighbour as yourself.
(Mark 12:31, NIV)

Two duties

(Saint Teresa of Avila in a letter to her nuns pointed out that discovering our love to our neighbour is the surest sign of discovering our love to God.)

There are only two duties which our Lord requires of us, namely, the love of God, and the love of our neighbour. In my opinion, the surest sign for discovery whether we observe these two duties, is the love of our neighbour; since we cannot know whether we love God, though we may have strong proof of it; but this can be more easily discovered respecting the love of our neighbour. And be assured that the more you advance in the love of your neighbour, the more you advance in the love of God. . . . But alas! How many worms lie gnawing at the roots of our love to our neighbour! Self-love, self-esteem, fault-finding, envy, anger, impatience, and scorn. I assure you I write this with great grief, seeing myself to be so miserable a sinner against all my neighbours.

St Teresa of Avila, *Letters*

Where there is love, there is God.

Traditional saying, based on 1 John 4:12

Love for the whole human race

Because our Saviour has shown in the parable of the good Samaritan (Luke 10:36) that the term 'neighbour' includes the most distant stranger, there is no excuse for limiting the maxim of love to our own circle. Of course, the closer the relation, the more frequent our acts of kindness should be.

Our human situation leads to more ties in common between those who are linked by relationship, friendship or neighbourhood. This is acceptable to God; indeed, his plan for mankind makes it inevitable. Nevertheless, we must embrace the whole human race in our charitable feelings.

God demands that the love we bear to him should be spread abroad among all mankind. Our basic principle must always be that whatever a person may be like, we must still love him, because we love God.

John Calvin, *The Institutes of Christian Religion*

You are as prone to love as the sun is to shine, it being the most delightful and natural employment of the soul of man, without which you are dark and miserable. Consider therefore the extent of love, its vigour and excellency. For certainly he that delights not in love makes vain the universe, and is of necessity to himself the greatest burden.

Thomas Traherne, *Centuries*

Love one another

Three things are necessary for those who aim to follow the way of prayer – so necessary that, even if one is not much of a contemplative, they will help one forward greatly in the service of the Lord; and it is not possible to be much of a contemplative without them. Those who think they are, are badly deceived. The first is love for one another; the second is emotional detachment from all created things; the third is true humility.

St Teresa of Avila, *The Way of Perfection*

TODAY

TODAY – Mend a quarrel. Search out a forgotten friend. Dismiss suspicion and replace it with trust. Write a love letter. Share some treasure. Give a soft answer. Encourage youth. Manifest your loyalty in a word or a deed.

TODAY – Keep a promise. Find the time. Forgo a grudge. Forgive an enemy. Listen. Apologise if you were wrong. Try to understand. Flout envy. Examine your demands on others. Think first of someone else. Appreciate, be kind, be gentle. Laugh a little more.

TODAY – Deserve confidence. Take up arms against malice. Decry complacency. Express your gratitude. Worship your God. Gladden the heart of a child. Take pleasure in the beauty and wonder of the earth. Speak it again. Speak it still again. Speak it still once again.

Anonymous

Tenderness towards all creatures

I believe where the love of God is truly perfected, and the true spirit of government watchfully attended to, a tenderness towards all creatures made subject to us will be experienced; and a care felt in us, that we do not lessen that sweetness of life in the animal creation, which the great Creator intends for them under our government.

To say we love God as unseen, and at the same time exercise cruelty toward the least creature moving by his life, or by life derived from him, was a contradiction in itself.

John Woolman, *Journal*

Love and pets

Let every creature have your love. Love, with its fruits of meekness, patience, and humility, is all that we can wish for to ourselves, and our fellow-creatures; for this is to live in God, united to him, both for time and eternity. To desire to communicate good to every creature, in the degree we can, and it is capable of receiving from us, is a divine temper; for thus God stands unchangeably disposed towards the whole creation.

William Law, *A Serious Call to a Devout and Holy Life*

Seek Love in the pity of others' woe

Seek Love in the pity of others' woe,
In the gentle relief of another's care,
In the darkness of night and the winter's snow,
In the naked and outcast, seek Love there.
William Blake

A meditation on 1 Corinthians 13:13

'And now these three remain: faith, hope and love. But the greatest of these is love.'

He who has charity is not jealous, nor envious, neither does he speak evil of his neighbour. He does not rejoice at the fall of others; he does not criminate the fallen, but he sorrows with him, and does what he can to comfort him. He does not pass by his brother in adversity; but he aids him, and even dies with him. He who has charity does the will of God, and learns of Him; for our own good Master Himself said: 'By this shall all men know that ye are my disciples, if you have love one to another.' He that has charity thinks no one a stranger; but he looks upon all men as his own kindred. He that has charity endures all things, is long-suffering, and kind to all. Truly may we say that 'God is love, and he that dwelleth in love dwelleth in God.'

St Ephraim Syrus, *Meditations*

Watchfulness in little things

Our Lord asks but two things of us

Our Lord asks but two things of us: Love for him and for our neighbour: this is what we must strive to obtain. Be sure that as you make progress in brotherly love you are increasing in your love for God. In this most important matter we should be most watchful in little things, and take no notice of the great works we plan during prayer.

St Teresa of Avila, *Conception on the Love of God*

Little things out of love

We should, once and for all, he said, entrust ourselves to God, abandon ourselves to him alone, confident that he would not deceive us. We must not grow weary in doing little things for the love of God, who looks not on the greatness of the deed, but to the love of the deed.

Brother Lawrence, *The Practice of the Presence of God*

Loving people you hate

You will find all that is lacking in your heart in the heart of Jesus, dying on the cross. Then you will be enabled to love those whom you would naturally, in your pride, hate and crush.

François Fénelon, *Christian Perfection*

Whatever a person may be like, we must still love him, because we love God.

John Calvin, *The Institutes of Christian Religion*

Hate stirs up trouble, but love overlooks all offences.

Proverbs 10:12, GNB

If your enemies are hungry, feed them; if they are thirsty, give them a drink. You will make them burn with shame, and the LORD will reward you.

Proverbs 25:21–2, GNB

You have heard that it was said, 'Love your friends, hate your enemies.' But now I tell you: love your enemies and pray for those who persecute you.

Matthew 5:43–4, GNB

Act as if you loved

Don't waste time bothering about whether you love your neighbour; act as if you did. As soon as we do this we discover one of the great secrets. When you are behaving as if you love someone, you will presently come to love him. If you injure someone you dislike, you will find yourself disliking him more. If you do him a good turn, you will find yourself disliking him less.

C. S. Lewis, *Mere Christianity*

Be assured that the more you advance in the love of your neighbour, the more you advance in the love of God. . . . But alas! How many worms lie gnawing at the roots of our love to our neighbour! Self-love, self-esteem, fault-finding, envy, anger, impatience, and scorn. I assure you I write this with great grief, seeing myself to be so miserable a sinner against all my neighbours.

Teresa of Avila, *The Way of Perfection*

Participating in divine love

Charity is the great channel through which God passes all his mercy upon mankind. For we receive forgiveness of our sins in proportion to our forgiving our brother. This is the rule of our hopes, and the measure of our desire in this world; and in the day of death and judgment the great sentence upon mankind shall be transacted according to our alms, which is the other part of charity. Certain it is, that God cannot, will not, never did, reject a charitable man in his greatest needs and in his passionate prayers; for God himself is love, and every degree of charity that dwells in us is the participation of the divine nature.

Jeremy Taylor, *Holy Living, Holy Dying*

Loving difficult people

God is the first object of our love: its next office is to bear the defects of others. And we should begin the practice of this amid our own household.

John Wesley, *A Plain Man's Guide to Holiness*

Kindness

Kindness is a language which the blind can see and the deaf can hear.
Author unknown

A religion which does not make us kind is not our Lord's religion.
Anonymous, *The Christlike Christian*

Pure love

An instant of pure love is more precious to God and the soul, and more profitable to the church, than all other good works together, though it may seem as if nothing were done.
St John of the Cross, *The Dark Night of the Soul*

God regards with how much love a person performs a work, rather than how much he does.
The Imitation of Christ, ascribed to Thomas à Kempis

Our Lord does not care so much for the importance of our works as for the love with which they are done.
St Teresa of Avila, *Exclamation of the Soul to God*

True affection is ingeniously inventive.
François Fénelon, *Christian Perfection*

Take the opportunity

Love cannot be practised right unless we first exercise it in the moment God gives the opportunity; and second, we cease the instant after to offer it to God by humble thanksgiving.

John Wesley, *The Plain Man's Guide to Holiness*

I want to teach people who live in crowded cities within their families, in the middle of domestic cares at home or in the press of public affairs in their professional life. It is a mistake, even a heresy, to want to banish the devout life from the soldier's camp, the manual worker's workshop, the court of princes, the homes of married people.

St François de Sales, *Introduction to the Devout Life*

Stop one heart from breaking

If I can stop one heart from breaking,
I shall not live in vain;
If I can ease one life the aching,
Or cool one pain,
Or help one fainting robin
Unto his nest again,
I shall not live in vain.

Emily Dickinson

If anyone gives even a cup of cold water to one of these little ones because he is my disciple, I tell you the truth, he will certainly not lose his reward.

Matthew 10:42, NIV

Love never ends

If we turn our minds towards the good, it is impossible that little by little the whole soul will not be attracted thereto in spite of itself.

Simone Weil, *Waiting on God*

It is our care for the helpless, our practice of lovingkindness, that brands us in the eyes of many of our opponents. 'Look!' they say. 'How they love one another! Look they are prepared to die for one another.'

Tertullian, *Letters*

PART FIVE

LOVE AND MARRIAGE

May you rejoice in the wife of your youth.
. . . May you ever be captivated by her love.
(Proverbs 5:18–19, NIV)

A wife to a husband

How do I love thee? Let me count the ways.
I love thee to the depth and breadth and height
My soul can reach, when feeling out of sight
For the end of Being and ideal Grace.
I love thee to the level of everyday's
Most quiet need, by sun and candlelight.
I love thee freely, as men strive for Right;
I love thee purely, as they turn from Praise.
I love thee with the passion put to use
In my old griefs, and with my childhood's faith.
I love thee with a love I seemed to lose
With my lost saints, – I love thee with the breath,
Smiles, tears, of all my life! – and, if God choose,
I shall but love thee better after death.
Elizabeth Barrett Browning

Shall I compare thee to a summer's day?

Shall I compare thee to a summer's day?
  Thou art more lovely and more temperate:
Rough winds do shake the darling buds of May,
  And summer's lease hath all too short a date:
Sometime too hot the eye of heaven shines,
  And often is his gold complexion dimmed;
And every fair from fair sometime declines,
  By chance, or nature's changing course untrimmed;
But thy eternal summer shall not fade,
  Nor lose possession of that fair thou owest,
Nor shall death brag thou wanderest in his shade,
  When in eternal lines to time thou growest;
    So long as men can breathe, or eyes can see,
    So long lives this, and this gives life to thee.

William Shakespeare, *Sonnets*

An ancient love poem

My lover is radiant and ruddy,
    outstanding among ten thousand.
His head is purest gold;
    his hair is wavy
    and black as raven.
His eyes are like doves
    by the water streams,
    washed in milk,
    mounted like jewels.
His cheeks are like beds of spice
    yielding perfume.
His lips are like lilies
    dripping with myrrh.
His arms are rods of gold
    set with chrysolite.
His body is like polished ivory
    decorated with sapphires.
His legs are pillars of marble
    set on bases of pure gold.
His appearance is like Lebanon,
    choice as its cedars.
His mouth is sweetness itself;
    he is altogether lovely.
This is my lover, this my friend,
    O daughters of Jerusalem.

Song of Songs 5:10–16, NIV

Song of Songs

How beautiful your sandalled feet,
   O prince's daughter!
Your graceful legs are like jewels,
   the work of a craftsman's hands.
Your navel is a rounded goblet
   that never lacks blended wine.
Your waist is a mound of wheat
   encircled by lilies.
Your breasts are like two fawns,
   twins of a gazelle.
Your neck is like an ivory tower.
Your eyes are the pools of Heshbon
   by the gate of Bath Rabbim.
Your nose is like the tower of Lebanon
   looking towards Damascus.
Your head crowns you like Mount Carmel.
   Your hair is like royal tapestry;
   the king is held captive by its tresses.
How beautiful you are and how pleasing,
   O love, with your delights!
Your stature is like that of the palm,
   and your breasts like clusters of fruit.
I said, 'I will climb the palm tree;
   I will take hold of its fruit.'
May your breasts be like the clusters of the vine,
   the fragrance of your breath like apples,
   and your mouth like the best wine.

Song of Songs 7:1–9, NIV

God's purposes in marriage

A man will leave his father and mother and be united to his wife, and they will become one flesh.

Genesis 2:24, NIV

May your fountain be blessed,
    and may you rejoice in the wife of your youth.
A loving doe, a graceful deer –
    may her breasts satisfy you always,
    may you ever be captivated by her love.

Proverbs 5:18–19, NIV

Sons are a heritage from the LORD,
    children a reward from him.
Like arrows in the hands of a warrior
    are sons born in one's youth.
Blessed is the man
    whose quiver is full of them.

Psalm 127:3–5, NIV

Husbands, love your wives, just as Christ loved the church and gave himself up for her.

Ephesians 5:25, NIV

PART SIX

THE WAY OF LOVE

The fruit of the Spirit is love.
(Galatians 5:22, NIV)

Love is

Love is swift,
pure,
meek,
joyous and glad,
strong,
patient,
faithful,
wise,
forbearing,
manly,
and never seeketh himself or his own will;
for whensoever a man seeketh himself, he falleth from love.
    Also love is circumspect,
meek,
righteous;
nor heeding vain things;
sober,
chaste,
stable,
quiet,
and well stabled in his outward wits.

The Imitation of Christ, ascribed to Thomas à Kempis

John, the 'apostle of love'

For God so loved the world that he gave his one and only Son, that whoever believes in him shall not perish but have eternal life.

John 3:16, NIV

A new command I give you: Love one another. As I have loved you, so you must love one another. By this all men will know that you are my disciples, if you love one another.

John 13:34–5, NIV

As the Father has loved me, so have I loved you. Now remain in my love.

John 15:9, NIV

The Father himself loves you.

John 16:27, NIV

Love each other as I have loved you. Greater love has no-one than this, that he lay down his life for his friends.

John 15:12–13, NIV

How great is the love the Father has lavished on us, that we should be called children of God! And that is what we are!

1 John 3:1, NIV

Dear children, let us not love with words or tongue but with actions and in truth.

1 John 3:18, NIV

There is no fear in love. But perfect love drives out fear.

1 John 4:18, NIV

You have forsaken your first love. Remember the height from which you have fallen! Repent and do the things you did at first.

Revelation 2:4, NIV

This is how much God loves us

Dear friends, let us love one another, for love comes from God.
Everyone who loves has been born of God and knows God.
Whoever does not love does not know God, because God is
love.

This is how God showed his love among us:
He sent his one and only Son into the world that we might live
through him.
This is love:
not that we loved God,
but that he loved us
and sent his Son
as an atoning sacrifice for our sins.

Dear friends, since God so loved us,
we also ought to love one another.

No-one has ever seen God;
but if we love one another,
God lives in us
and his live is made complete in us.

1 John 4:7–12, NIV

Love is not love

Love is not love
That alters when it alteration finds
Or bends with the remover to remove:
Oh no! It is an ever fixed mark
That looks on tempests and is never shaken;
It is the star to every wandering bark
Whose worth's unknown, although his height be taken.
Love's not Time's fool, though rosy lips and cheeks
Within his bending sickle's compass come;
Love alters not with his brief hours and weeks
But bears it out even to the edge of doom.
William Shakespeare

To my God a heart of flame;
To my fellow man a heart of love;
To myself a heart of steel.
St Augustine, *The City of God*

The fruit of the Spirit is love

The fruit of the Spirit is love, joy, peace, patience, kindness, goodness, faithfulness, gentleness and self-control.
Galatians 5:22–3, NIV

You have heard that it was said, 'Eye for eye, and tooth for tooth.' But I tell you, Do not resist an evil person. If someone strikes you on the right cheek, turn to him the other also.
Matthew 5:38–9, NIV

In everything, do to others what you would have them do to you.
Matthew 7:12, NIV

Love must be sincere. Hate what is evil; cling to what is good.
Romans 12:9, NIV

Love does no harm to its neighbour.
Romans 13:10, NIV

Knowledge puffs up, but love builds up.
1 Corinthians 8:1, NIV

Do everything in love.
1 Corinthians 16:14, NIV

Be completely humble and gentle; be patient, bearing with one another in love.
Ephesians 4:2, NIV

Love one another deeply, from the heart.
1 Peter 1:22, NIV

Live in harmony with one another; be sympathetic, love as brothers, be compassionate and humble.
1 Peter 3:8, NIV

Love is better than to be loved

The more we love the better we are; and the greater our friendships are, the dearer we are to God.

Jeremy Taylor, *Holy Living, Holy Dying*

Holy, heavenly love

Gracious Spirit, Holy Ghost,
Taught by thee, we covet most
Of thy gifts at Pentecost,
Holy, heavenly love.

Love is kind, and suffers long,
Love is meek, and thinks no wrong,
Love than death itself more strong;
Therefore give us love.

Prophecy will fade away,
Melting in the light of day;
Love will ever with us stay;
Therefore give us love.

Faith will vanish into sight;
Hope be emptied in delight;
Love in heaven will shine more bright;
Therefore give us love.

Faith and hope and love we see
Joining hand in hand agree;
But the greatest of the three,
And the best, is love.

From the overshadowing
Of thy gold and silver wing
Shed on us, who to thee sing,
Holy, heavenly love.

Christopher Wordsworth

Love and do what you will

All things are possible to him who believes, yet more to him who hopes, more still to him who loves, and most of all to him who practises and perseveres in these three virtues.
Brother Lawrence, *The Practice of the Presence of God*

Love is the abridgement of all theology.
St François de Sales, *Introduction to a Devout Life*

Love and do what you will.
St Augustine, *Confessions*

They who will learn love, will always be its scholars.
Byron, *Don Juan*

1 Corinthians 13

Love is patient, love is kind. It does not envy, it does not boast, it is not proud. It is not rude, it is not self-seeking, it is not easily angered, it keeps no records of wrongs. Love does not delight in evil but rejoices with the truth. It always protects, always trusts, always hopes, always perseveres.

Love never fails. But where there are prophecies, they will cease; where there are tongues, they will be stilled; where there is knowledge, it will pass away. For we know in part and we prophesy in part, but when perfection comes, the imperfect disappears. When I was a child, I talked like a child, I thought like a child, I reasoned like a child. When I became a man, I put childish ways behind me. Now we see but a poor reflection as in a mirror; then we shall see face to face. Now I know in part; then I shall know fully, even as I am fully known.

And now these three remain: faith, hope and love. But the greatest of these is love.

1 Corinthians 13:4–13, NIV

With the Lord

Brothers, we do not want you to be ignorant about those who fall asleep, or to grieve like the rest of men, who have no hope. We believe that Jesus died and rose again and so we believe that God will bring with Jesus those who have fallen asleep in him. According to the Lord's own word, we tell you that we who are still alive, who are left till the coming of the Lord, will certainly not precede those who have fallen asleep. For the Lord himself will come down from heaven, with a loud command, with the voice of the archangel and with the trumpet call of God, and the dead in Christ will rise first. After that, we who are still alive and are left will be caught up together with them in the clouds to meet the Lord in the air. And so we will be with the Lord for ever. Therefore encourage each other with these words.

1 Thessalonians 4:13–18, NIV

BIOGRAPHICAL NOTES

Aelred (1110–1163), abbot of the 600-strong Cistercian monastery at Rievaulx in Yorkshire

St **Bernard** (1090–1153), abbot of Clairvaux who wrote a monastic Rule and several mystical treatises

Bianco da Siena (14th century), Italian spiritual writer

William Blake (1757–1827), English engraver and visionary poet

St **Bonaventura** (1221–1274), Italian Franciscan theologian

Elizabeth Barrett Browning (1806–1861), English poet; wife of Robert Browning

Lord **Byron** (1788–1824), English poet

John Calvin (1509–1564), Reformation theologian

Edward Caswall (1814–1878), translator of many Latin hymns

St **Catherine of Siena** (1347–1380), Italian mystic noted for her ecstatic prayer and her gift of reconciliation

John Clare (1793–1864), English poet

Samuel Crossman (1624–1683), English hymn-writer

Emily Dickinson (1830–1886), U.S. poet

Meister Eckhart (1260?–1327), German mystic and Dominican preacher

St **Ephraim Syrus** (306–373), deacon of Edessa in Syria

François Fénelon (1651–1715), Archbishop of Cambrai, who wrote many letters of spiritual guidance

Phineas Fletcher (1582–1650), English poet

St Francis of Assisi (1181–1226), Italian friar, who founded the Franciscan order

St François de Sales (1567–1622), bishop of Geneva and opponent of Calvin

Paul Gerhardt (1607–1676), German hymn-writer

Frances Ridley Havergal (1836–1879), English hymn-writer

George Herbert (1593–1633), English clergyman and poet

Walter Hilton (?–1396), English mystic

W. Walsham How (1823–1897), bishop of Wakefield

Jacopone da Todi (Jacopo Benedetti) (1230?–1306), Franciscan poet who probably wrote the Stabat Mater

John of Ruysbroeck (1293–1381), Flemish Augustinian mystic

St John of the Cross (1542–1591), Spanish mystic

Lady **Julian of Norwich** (c.1342–after 1413), English anchoress

John Keble (1792–1866), English poet and Tractarian

William Law (1686–1761), English clergyman and spiritual adviser

Brother **Lawrence** (1605–1691), French Carmelite lay brother and mystic

C. S. Lewis (1898–1963), English literary critic and Christian writer

Louis of Blois (Blosius) (?–1566) Benedictine abbot

Henry Martyn (1781–1812), English missionary and Bible translator

John Newton (1725–1807), English evangelical clergyman and hymn-writer

Blaise Pascal (1623–1662), French mathematician and theologian

Richard of St-Victor (?–1173), mystic and theologian of the Paris abbey of St-Victor

Richard Rolle (1300?–1349), English mystic

William Shakespeare (1564–1616), English dramatist

Johann Tauler (1300–1361), German mystic and Dominican, successor to Eckhart

Jeremy Taylor (1613–1667), Anglican bishop of Down and Connor

St Teresa of Avila (1515–1582), Spanish Carmelite mystic

Tertullian (150?–212?), North African theologian

Thomas à Kempis (1380?–1471), German devotional theologian who probably wrote *The Imitation of Christ*

Thomas Traherne (1636?–1674), English poet

Isaac Watts (1674–1748), English hymn-writer

Simone Weil (1909–1943), French philosopher and mystic

Charles Wesley (1707–1788), English clergyman and hymn-writer

John Wesley (1703–1791), English clergyman, founder of Methodism

John Woolman (1720–1772), US Quaker preacher and abolitionist

Christopher Wordsworth (1807–1885), bishop of Lincoln